Suicide and Self-harm

Vol. 87

Edited by Christina Hughes

Series Editor: Cara Acred

Independence Educational Publishers

First published by Independence
The Studio, High Green, Great Shelford
Cambridge CB22 5EG
England

British Library Cataloguing in Publication Data

Suicide and self-harm. -- (Issues today ; 87)

1. Self-mutilation--Juvenile literature. 2. Suicide--

Juvenile literature.

I. Series II. Acred, Cara editor.

616.8'582-dc23

ISBN-13: 9781861686831

Acknowledgements

The publisher is grateful for permission to reproduce the material in this book. While every care has been taken to trace and acknowledge copyright, the publisher tenders its apology for any accidental infringement or where copyright has proved untraceable. The publisher would be pleased to come to a suitable arrangement in any such case with the rightful owner.

Illustrations

All illustrations, including the cover, are by Don Hatcher.

Images

Page 9: MorgueFile, page 12: Unsplash.

Editorial by Christina Hughes and layout by Jackie Staines, on behalf of Independence Educational Publishers.

Printed in Great Britain by MWL Print Group Ltd.

Cara Acred

Cambridge

May 2014

Contents

Chapter 1: Self-harm

Chapter 2: Suicide

About this book

Suicide and Self-harm is Volume 87 in the ***ISSUES* today** series.

A recent study found that 43% of young people know someone who has self-harmed. However, one in four would not know what to say to a friend who was self-harming. In addition to this frightening statistic, 4,400 people end their own lives in England each year – that's one death every two hours. This book deals with the highly-emotive topics of self-harm and suicide in a sensitive and carefully thought-out manner, using up-to-date statistics and real-life experiences. It also examines coping mechanisms for those who self-harm and looks at methods of suicide prevention and intervention.

Suicide and Self-harm offers a useful overview of the many issues involved in this topic. However, at the end of each article is a URL for the relevant organisation's website, which can be visited by pupils who want to carry out further research.

Because the information in this book is gathered from a number of different sources, pupils should think about the origin of the text and critically evaluate the information that is presented. Does the source have a particular bias or agenda? Are you being presented with facts or opinions? Do you agree with the writer?

At the end of each chapter there are two pages of activities relating to the articles and issues raised in that chapter. The 'Brainstorm' questions can be done as a group or individually after reading the articles. This should prompt some ideas and lead on to further activities. Some suggestions for such activities are given under the headings 'Oral', 'Moral dilemmas', 'Research', 'Written' and 'Design' that follow the 'Brainstorm' questions.

For more information about ***ISSUES* today** and its sister series, ***ISSUES*** (for pupils aged 14 to 18), please visit the Independence website.

About *ISSUES* today

***ISSUES* today** is a series of resource books on contemporary social issues, designed for Key Stage 3 pupils and above. This series is also suitable for Scottish P7, S1 and S2 students.

Each volume contains information from a variety of sources, including government reports and statistics, newspaper and magazine articles, surveys and polls, academic research and literature from charities and lobby groups. The information has been tailored to an 11 to 14 age group; it has been rewritten and presented in a simple, straightforward and accessible format.

In addition, each ***ISSUES* today** title features handy tasks and assignments based on the information contained in the book, for use in class, for homework or as a revision aid.

***ISSUES* today** can be used as a learning resource in a variety of Key Stage 3 subjects, including English, Science, History, Geography, PSHE, Citizenship, Sex and Relationships Education and Religious Education.

WARNING

This book contains sensitive material and may act as a trigger if you suffer from self-harming urges or suicidal thoughts.

www.independence.co.uk

Self-harm

What is self-harm?

Self-harm happens when you hurt or harm yourself. You may:

- take too many tablets – an overdose
- cut yourself
- burn yourself
- bang your head or throw yourself against something hard
- punch yourself
- stick things in your body
- swallow things.

How common is self-harm?

- About one in ten young people will self-harm at some point, but it can happen at any age.
- The research probably underestimates how common self-harm is. It is usually based on surveys of people who go to hospital or their GP after harming themselves. However, we know that a lot of people do not seek help after self-harm. Some types of self-harm, like cutting, may be more secret and so less likely to be noticed.
- In a recent study of over 4,000 self-harming adults in hospital, 80% had overdosed and around 15% had cut themselves. In the community, it is likely that cutting is a more common way of self-harming than taking an overdose.

Who self-harms?

It happens more often in:

- young women
- prisoners, asylum seekers and veterans of the armed forces
- gay, lesbian and bisexual people: this seems, at least in part, due to the stress of prejudice and discrimination
- a group of young people who self-harm together: having a friend who self-harms may increase your chances of doing it as well
- people who have experienced physical, emotional or sexual abuse during childhood.

What makes people self-harm?

Research has shown that many people who harm themselves are struggling with intolerable distress or unbearable situations. A person will often struggle with difficulties for some time before they self-harm.

Common problems include:

- physical or sexual abuse
- feeling depressed
- feeling bad about yourself
- relationship problems with partners, friends and family
- being unemployed or having difficulties at work.

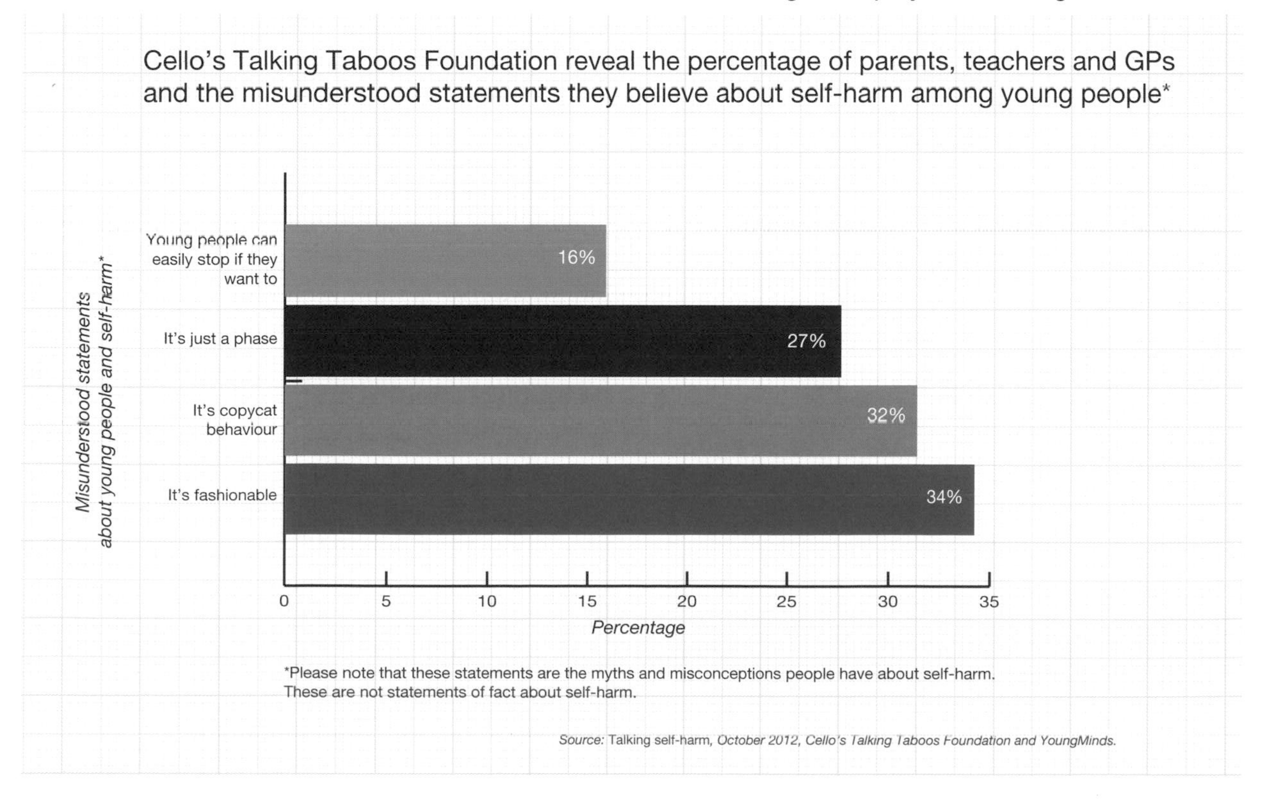

You may be more likely to harm yourself if you feel:

- that people don't listen to you
- hopeless
- isolated, alone
- out of control
- powerless – it feels as though there's nothing you can do to change anything.

It's more likely to happen if you are using alcohol or drugs – it may feel that these are as out of control as the rest of your life.

You may feel like harming yourself if you want to show someone else how distressed you are or to get back at them or to punish them. This is not common – most people suffer in silence and self-harm in private.

What help is there?

Talking with a non-professional

You may find it helpful just to talk anonymously to someone else about what is happening to you. Knowing that someone else knows what you are going through can help you to feel less alone with your problems. It can also help you to think about your difficulties more clearly – maybe even see ways of solving them that you wouldn't think of on your own. You can do this on the Internet or by telephone. Telephone helplines are listed at the end of this article.

Self-help groups

A group of people, who all self-harm, meet regularly to give each other emotional support and practical advice. Just sharing your problems in a group can help you to feel less alone – others in the group will almost certainly have had similar experiences.

Talking with a professional

One-to-one talking treatments can help, such as:

- Problem-solving therapy
- Cognitive behavioural therapy
- Psychodynamic psychotherapy
- Family meetings.

If you are still living with your family, it may help to have a family meeting with a therapist. This can help to relieve the tiring, daily stress for everyone in the family. It is not always appropriate, for instance, if you are the victim of physical or sexual abuse within your family.

Group therapy

This is different from a self-help group. A professional will lead (or facilitate) the group to help the members to deal with problems they share; for example, in getting on with other people.

What works best?

There isn't much good evidence yet of which therapies work well for people who have harmed themselves. However, what evidence there is, suggests that problem-solving therapy and cognitive behavioural therapy are useful. A health professional will make suggestions based on your individual problems and on what is available locally.

What if I don't get help?

About one in three people who self-harm for the first time will do it again during the following year.

- About three in 100 people who self-harm over 15 years will actually kill themselves. This is more than 50 times the rate for people who don't self-harm. The risk increases with age and is much greater for men.
- Cutting can give you permanent scarring. If nerves or tendons are damaged by cutting, this can lead to numbness or weakness.

How can I help myself?

The feelings of self-harm will go away after a while. If you can cope with your distress without self-harming for a time, it will get easier over the next few hours. You can:

- Talk to someone – if you are on your own perhaps you could phone a friend. Telephone helplines are listed at the end of this article.
- If the person you are with is making you feel worse, go out.
- Distract yourself by going out, listening to music or by doing something harmless that interests you.
- Relax and focus your mind on something pleasant – your very own personal comforting place.
- Find another way to express your feelings such as squeezing ice cubes (which you can make with red juice to mimic blood if the sight of blood is important) or just drawing red lines on your skin.
- Give yourself some 'harmless pain' – eat a hot chilli or have a cold shower.
- Focus your mind on positive things.
- Be kind to yourself – allow yourself to do something harmless that you enjoy.
- Write a diary or a letter to explain what is happening to you – no one else needs to see it.

When you don't feel like harming yourself

When the urge has gone, and you feel safe, think about the times that you have self-harmed and what (if anything) has been helpful.

- Go back in your mind to the last time when you did not want to self-harm and move forward in your memory from there.

DID YOU KNOW

Speak up

Did you know that there are a number of free confidential helplines that offer advice and support? If you're worried about yourself or someone you know, these self-help phone lines are there to listen. See below for more details.

- Think about where you were, who you were with and what you were feeling.
- Try to work out why you began feeling like you did.
- Did your self-harm give you a sense of escape, or relief or control? Try to work out something to do that might give you the same result, but that doesn't damage you.
- How did other people react?
- Could you have done anything else?
- Make an audio recording. Talk about your good points and why you don't want to self-harm. Or, ask someone you trust to do this. When you start to feel bad, you can play this back to remind yourself of the parts of you that are good and worthwhile.
- Make a 'crisis plan' so you can talk to someone instead of self-harming. Being able to get in touch with someone quickly can help you control your urge to self-harm. While you are talking, your wish to harm yourself may start to go away.

Self-help and support

ChildLine

Free national helpline for young people, free confidential advice on all sorts of problems: 0800 1111.

Samaritans

Telephone and e-mail support for anyone who is worried, upset or suicidal; 08457 90 90 90; ROI 1850 60 90 90; e-mail: jo@samaritans.org.

NHS Direct

A helpline with health advice – now call either 0845 4647 (depending on your area) or 111.

January 2012

www.rcpsych.ac.uk/healthadvice/problemsdisorders.aspx

Self-harm and cutting

Self-injury help, support and treatment.

Self-harm can be a way of coping with problems. It may help you express feelings you can't put into words, distract you from your life or release emotional pain. Afterwards, you probably feel better – at least for a little while. But then the painful feelings return and you feel the urge to hurt yourself again. If you want to stop but don't know how, remember this: you deserve to feel better and you can get there without hurting yourself.

'Remember this: you deserve to feel better and you can get there without hurting yourself.'

Understanding cutting and self-harm

Self-harm is a way of expressing and dealing with deep distress and emotional pain. As counter-intuitive as it may sound to those on the outside, hurting yourself makes you feel better. In fact, you may feel like you have no choice. Injuring yourself is the only way you know how to cope with feelings like sadness, self-loathing, emptiness, guilt and rage.

The problem is that the relief that comes from self-harming doesn't last very long. It's like slapping on a plaster when what you really need are stitches. It may temporarily stop the bleeding, but it doesn't fix the underlying injury. And it also creates its own problems.

'The problem is that the relief that comes from self-harming doesn't last very long. It's like slapping on a plaster when what you really need are stitches.'

If you're like most people who self-injure, you try to keep what you're doing secret. Maybe you feel ashamed or maybe you just think that no one would understand. But hiding who you are and what you feel is a heavy burden. Ultimately, the secrecy and guilt affects your relationships with your friends and family members and the way you feel about yourself. It can make you feel even more lonely, worthless and trapped.

Myths and facts about cutting and self-harm

Because cutting and other means of self-harm tend to be taboo subjects, the people around you – and possibly even you – may harbour serious misconceptions about your motivations and state of mind. Don't let these myths get in the way of getting help or helping someone you care about.

People who cut and self-injure are trying to get attention

Fact: The painful truth is that people who self-harm generally do so in secret. They aren't trying to manipulate others or draw attention to themselves. In fact, shame and fear can make it very difficult to come forward and ask for help.

People who self-injure are crazy and/or dangerous

Fact: It is true that many people who self-harm suffer from anxiety, depression or a previous trauma – just like millions of others in the general population. Self-injury is how they cope. Slapping them with a 'crazy' or 'dangerous' label isn't accurate or helpful.

People who self-injure want to die

Fact: Self-injurers usually do not want to die. When they self-harm, they are not trying to kill themselves – they are trying to cope with their pain. In fact, self-injury may be a way of helping themselves go on living. However, in the long-term, people who self-injure have a much higher risk of suicide, which is why it's so important to seek help.

If the wounds aren't bad, it's not that serious

Fact: The severity of a person's wounds has very little to do with how much he or she may be suffering. Don't assume that because the wounds or injuries are minor, there's nothing to worry about.

Signs and symptoms of cutting and self-harm

Self-harm includes anything you do to intentionally injure yourself. Some of the more common ways include:

- cutting or severely scratching your skin
- burning or scalding yourself
- hitting yourself or banging your head
- punching things or throwing your body against walls and hard objects
- sticking objects into your skin
- intentionally preventing wounds from healing
- swallowing poisonous substances or inappropriate objects.

Self-harm can also include less obvious ways of hurting yourself or putting yourself in danger, such as driving recklessly, binge drinking, taking too many drugs and having unsafe sex.

Warning signs that a family member or friend is cutting or self-injuring

Because clothing can hide physical injuries, and inner struggle can be covered up by acting calm, self-injury can be hard to detect. However, there are red flags you can look for (but remember – you don't have to be sure that you know what's going on in order to reach out to someone you're worried about):

- Unexplained wounds or scars from cuts, bruises or burns, usually on the wrists, arms, thighs or chest.
- Blood stains on clothing, towels or bedding; blood-soaked tissues.
- Sharp objects or cutting instruments, such as razors, knives, needles, glass shards or bottle caps, in the person's belongings.
- Frequent 'accidents'. Someone who self-harms may claim to be clumsy or have many mishaps, in order to explain away injuries.
- Covering up. A person who self-injures may insist on wearing long sleeves or long pants, even in hot weather.
- Needing to be alone for long periods of time, especially in the bedroom or bathroom.
- Isolation and irritability.

How does cutting and self-harm help?

It's important to acknowledge that self-harm helps you – otherwise you wouldn't do it. Some of the ways cutting and self-harming can help include:

- Expressing feelings you can't put into words
- Releasing the pain and tension you feel inside
- Helping you feel in control
- Distracting you from overwhelming emotions or difficult life circumstances
- Relieving guilt and punishing yourself
- Making you feel alive, or simply feel something, instead of feeling numb.

Once you better understand why you self-harm, you can learn ways to stop self-harming and find resources that can support you through this struggle.

If self-harm helps, why stop?

- Although self-harm and cutting can give you temporary relief, it comes at a cost. In the long term, it causes far more problems than it solves.
- The relief is short lived and is quickly followed by other feelings like shame and guilt. Meanwhile, it keeps you from learning more effective strategies for feeling better.
- Keeping the secret from friends and family members is difficult and lonely.
- You can hurt yourself badly, even if you don't mean to. It's easy to misjudge the depth of a cut or end up with an infected wound.
- If you don't learn other ways to deal with emotional pain, it puts you at risk for bigger problems down the line, including major depression, drug and alcohol addiction and suicide.
- Self-harm can become addictive. It may start off as an impulse or something you do to feel more in control, but soon it feels like the cutting or self-harming is controlling you. It often turns into a compulsive behaviour that seems impossible to stop.

The bottom line: self-harm and cutting don't help you with the issues that made you want to hurt yourself in the first place.

Mini glossary

Counter-intuitive *– contrary to what common sense tells you is correct.*

The above information is reprinted with kind permission from Helpguide.

www.helpguide.org

The truth about self-harm

By Rebecca Whitefoot

Self-harmers are attention-seeking, manipulative teenagers. Self-harmers are suicidal. Self-harmers are goths. Self-harmers can stop if they want to. Self-harm is when you cut yourself with a knife. Myth. Myth. Myth. Myth. Myth!

How have we ended up getting it so wrong when it comes to sorting out self-harm fact from fiction?

Self-harm has a stigma that just won't budge. This is largely due to a lack of education and information available in schools and the NHS. In the Samaritans report *Youth Matters – A Cry For Help,* 43% of young people knew someone who has self-harmed, but one in four didn't know what to say to a friend who was self-harming.

We have the highest level of self-harm in Europe. Around 25,000 11- to 25-year-olds are admitted to Accident and Emergency each year in England because of self-harming. Of course this number is nowhere near the actual amount of people who harm themselves, because many people will administer first-aid at home and never seek help.

Statistics show a worrying imbalance. An estimated one in 12 young adults has cut themselves, a massive percentage, and yet education on prevention, support and recovery of self-harm just isn't there. In the same report by the Samaritans, 41% of young people believed that self-harm was selfish and 55% of people thought it was stupid. It's time we got informed about an issue that can wreak havoc on an individual's life, influencing everything from what they wear, to the relationships they have. We need to ask ourselves why there is such a large problem in the UK.

The motivations and methods used differ from one person to the next. Self-harm can be defined as burning, scalding, stabbing, banging heads and other body parts against walls, hair pulling, biting, breaking bones, jumping from heights or in front of vehicles and swallowing or inserting objects.

Self-harmers may also overdose with medicine(s) or poisonous substances. This is called self-poisoning.

There is no 'type' of person that self-harms. The onset can start at seven-years-old or at 50-years-old. And there is no one reason why a person begins. One reason may be that the individual feels issues in their life are out of control.

The act of self-harming can give that person a sense of control. They may be suffering with feelings of loneliness, isolation, stress and frustration. They may be battling with low self-esteem and poor body image. Work pressures, money worries and cultural and racial difficulties can all contribute. As do relationship problems, drug and alcohol issues, family breakdowns, bullying or bereavement.

One misconception, that needs to be dissolved, is that people who self-harm are trying to kill themselves. This is rarely the case as Frances McCann, a senior mental health practitioner explains, 'There's a big difference between someone saying they self-harm when they feel angry and a young person saying that they can't go on any more and want to end everything.'

The truth is the intention to commit suicide is only present in 15% of people. Self-harmers may harm to release their emotions. When the pressures of life become too high, self-harm becomes a safety valve – a way of relieving built-up tension. In an inquiry into self-harm published in the *Truth Hurts* report, 'a national inquiry into self-harm among young people', one respondent said, 'I don't deal with daily stress well, so when extra events occur, however big or small, my tension levels rise, resulting in my needing "release". Self-harm has proven to be most successful in this.'

The report found that after self-harming the person might feel calmer and more focused.

'It sounds awful but I felt I was a nicer person when I cut... balanced, normal.'

Self-harm can be an act of punishment in response to deep-rooted feelings of guilt and shame.

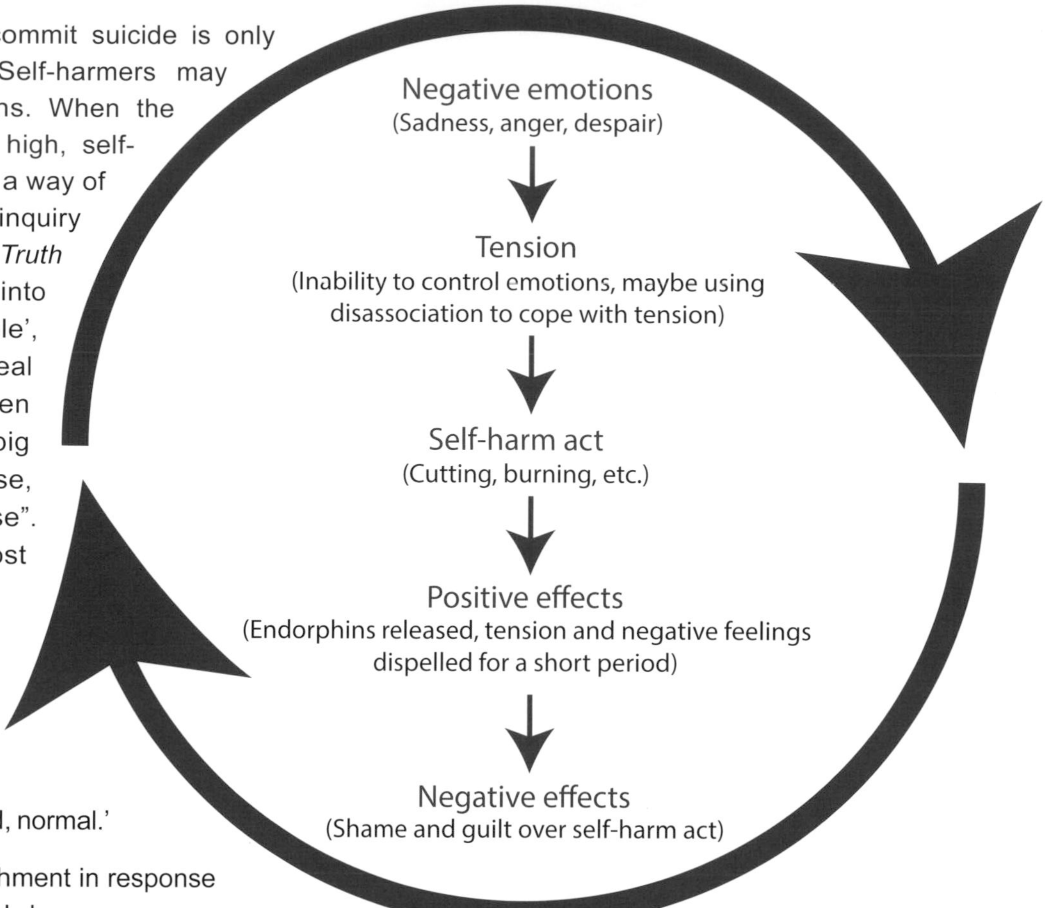

The pain of a cut can temporarily divert the individual's attention away from inner mental struggles. Sometimes it can feel like the blood is taking away all the bad feelings.

Some people said that self-harming made them feel reconnected with reality, 'Sometimes when I felt numb and empty, scratching myself helped me to feel emotions again. It brought me back to life again.'

Self-harmers can go to great lengths to cover their wounds, such as wearing long-sleeved tops or tights in sweltering conditions. However, if the wounds are on show some people see this as 'attention seeking'. This is yet another myth that must be banished.

Self-harmers find it immensely challenging to talk about their feelings of unhappiness and so they show their wounds as they feel this is the only way of communicating to other people how they're feeling inside and that they need help. As one self-harmer said, 'If someone's crying for help, don't stand there and judge the way in which they are asking for it.'

The inquiry also found that young people have been met with ridicule and hostility when they turned to professionals for help and that GPs are not sure how to approach the issue directly. Many self-harmers have had negative experiences when attending A & E.

'A & E isn't usually a positive experience. The last time I had a blood transfusion the consultant said I was wasting blood. The consultants there act as if to say, "Not you again".'

Many self-harmers will hide their activities from their family and friends because they are worried about the potential emotional impact. They fear their friends will view them differently once they've discussed their problems and in some instances, this becomes a reality.

Why are we, as a society, so worried about 'burdening' people with our problems? Why don't we talk more?

A self-harmer can feel guilt, shame and embarrassment about what they do to themselves. But why should self-harmers feel what they do is shameful or dirty when we accept eating disorders, alcoholism and drug abuse as serious mental conditions that require professional support and guidance?

Negative emotions
(Sadness, anger, despair)

↓

Tension
(Inability to control emotions, maybe using disassociation to cope with tension)

↓

Self-harm act
(Cutting, burning, etc.)

↓

Positive effects
(Endorphins released, tension and negative feelings dispelled for a short period)

↓

Negative effects
(Shame and guilt over self-harm act)

Source: Self-harm: information and suggestions for school and staff, *Children's Community Health Partnership, North Bristol NHS Trust, February 2011*

I spoke to a group of students at Winchester University about why they think the UK has such a high level of self-harm and why it still holds such a negative stigma.

One student said, 'I avoid discussing self-harm because I am afraid that I could be talking to someone who is in fact a self-harmer. It's the act of inflicting injury on yourself that is still so taboo.'

She went on to explain that self-harm was so common in our society but shrouded in secrecy. She said that this meant that a friend might be a self-harmer or have self-harmed and she wouldn't know. She said that, 'Alcoholism is more accepted than self-harm'. And that there are services such as Talk To Frank from which you can educate yourself about drugs, but there is no such service for self-harm.

Because of this lack of information those who disclose their problem to family and friends are often met with silence. The family and friends don't know how to respond since they are not educated on the subject.

Another student said that the 'go go go' work culture and fast-paced lifestyle in England makes people stressed and tense. Self-harm becomes an outlet for this tension. We need to slow down and ease off the pressures, they suggested.

Another student said we have adopted an 'American culture' in which everyone must be perfect and beautiful. Self-harm is an ugly blotch on this view and is therefore met with disapproval and disgust. She said we have put too high an expectation on ourselves and so when we can't cope with life it's like we have failed.

She added that films have a lot to answer for self-harm stereotypes. They do not portray self-harm in a realistic way, and often characters who self-harm will be 'goths' or 'stunningly beautiful teenagers' that glamourise the subject.

Thankfully steps are being made to get self-harm out there. A website, thesite.org, has recently launched a self-harm advice section, which is a fantastic resource for anyone affected.

The resource has been created by 42nd Street, Depaul UK and Youthnet (the charity that runs thesite.org), in response to the National Inquiry into self-harm.

Vera Martin, Director of 42nd Street, said, 'Self-harm is often misunderstood and frequently caricatured as attention seeking on the part of the young people who do it. But for many people self-harm is a response to – even a way of managing – deep-seated emotional distress and pain.'

For some people self-harm becomes an addictive cycle, a method of coping with the realities of our stressful, unpredictable lives. Breaking the cycle is tough, as the self-harmer will have to learn to go through the motions of hurt, anger, stress and grief without using that coping method. Self-harmers need the support and understanding of those around them.

We all have our own coping mechanisms. Some of us smoke, some of us drink alcohol, some of us exercise and some of us grab another bar of chocolate. Judging one person's coping method compared to another does not help. Getting to the bottom of why we need a coping mechanism in the first place is the key.

You can discover this by chatting to family, friends, going onto thesite.org discussion board or going to see a counsellor.

Talking about self-harm and informing yourself about it is the direction we all need to take to change the status of this stigma against self-harmers.

DID YOU KNOW

In most cases, people who self-harm do it to help themselves cope with unbearable and overwhelming emotional issues, caused by problems due to:

- *social factors – being bullied, having difficulties at work or school, or having difficult relationships with friends or family*
- *trauma – physical or sexual abuse, or the death of a close family member or friend*
- *mental health conditions – depression or borderline personality disorder*

Source: Self-harm, 29 July 2013, NHS Choices.

Mini glossary

Stigma *– something that has been branded with a negative view.*

The first time I said 'I self-harm'

Warning, some readers may find this post triggering.

Hi, my name is Suzi and I am a self-harmer but I am seven and a half years cut free. That's how I think of self-harming. I don't self-harm now but I am always in recovery, just like being in AA.

I started self-harming from a young age but it was at university that things unravelled for me. I found more and more that I was on a self-destructive path and the self-harming got worse. I seemed to start suffering from depression, I stopped going to lectures, I was smoking cannabis a lot, I was drinking a lot, I wasn't sleeping and my hair started to fall out.

My sister, who went to the same university, knew something wasn't right and did show concern but she didn't know the true extent of what was going on. I was in my second year of a law degree and there was no way I was going to pass the second year. My housemates noticed I was self-harming more and one of them tried to reach out to me. She sent me a beautiful card listing ten reasons why she loved me – it was hard to read. She finished the card by asking me not to hurt myself and added because it hurts her, to see me hurting. She never said it to my face or asked me, no one did.

The first time I said the words 'I self-harm'

I was encouraged to go and see my mentor – who was a university lecturer – and although I didn't explain everything, he suggested I talk to the doctor at uni. So I did. She said to put my second year on hold, I had to tell her exactly what was going on and why I was self-medicating with cannabis and alcohol. I didn't want to tell her but knew that she wouldn't be able to sign me off without giving her something. So the first time I said the words 'I self-harm' was to a random doctor. I wasn't enjoying my course and I wonder if I was ever destined to finish my law degree. But, I definitely was not in the best place to get the results I was capable of.

I was signed off for a year and was told I had to go for counselling to address the issues that were causing me to self-harm. I didn't go back to uni. I got a couple of jobs to keep me going and pay my rent. So I worked but I continued to drink too much and smoke cannabis and then I met someone. Who knew that nine years on we would be married! Things changed.

My boyfriend wasn't horrified or ashamed of me

Into the first year of our relationship, my then boyfriend, now husband, asked me what my scars were and why I did it. I didn't have an answer then but I did tell him what I did to myself. All of it. I laid it all bare for him to see my emotional nakedness. And he didn't go anywhere. So the first person I really confided in (the doctor didn't count), didn't run a mile. In fact, he wasn't horrified or ashamed of me. He was sad. He was sad that I felt I had to do it. He asked me to never do it again and to talk to him. And to be honest, I had a few slips in that first year or two, as I had nowhere to hide it from my boyfriend.

Taking the time to reflect on my life, I now understand why my family, who knew, didn't want to ask me why I did it and felt they couldn't ask me to stop: they were frightened of the answer. Or frightened that I would go off the rails and do it more. Or perhaps they were worried I would say it was because of them.

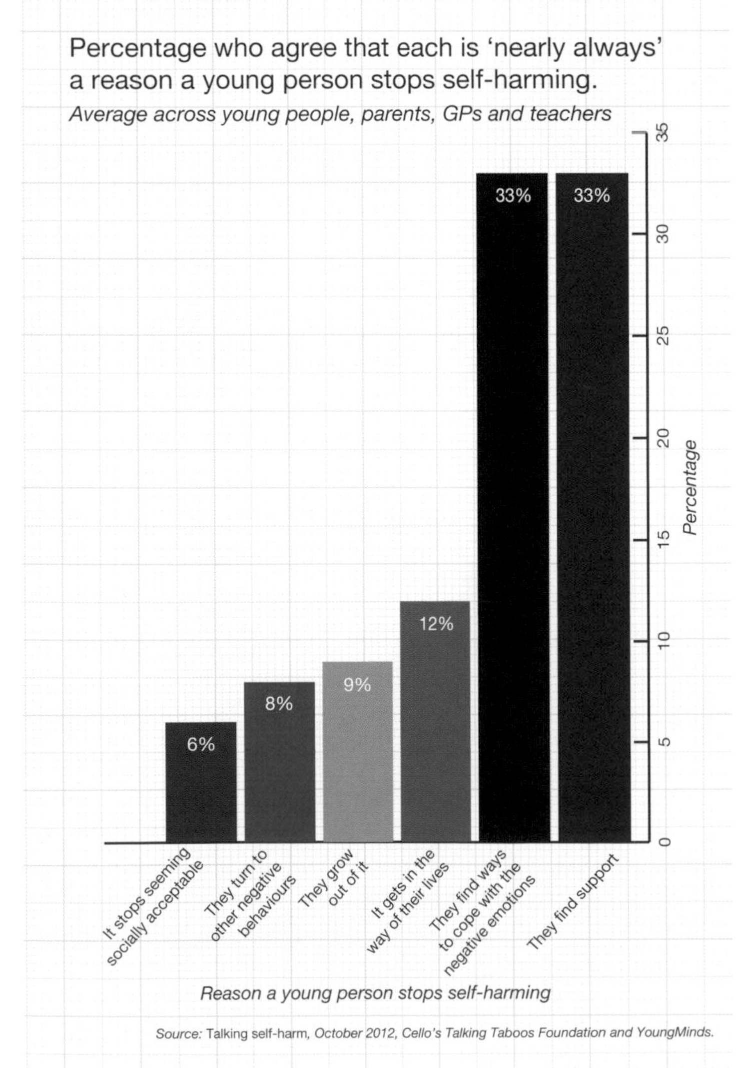

I can only now admit to myself why I did it

I know now that I self-harm to deal with my frustration and anger, usually at myself, and it started with my parents' divorce. Self-harming, for me, was a compulsion. I don't place any blame on anyone. Not even on myself. It was just my way of dealing with those feelings and it isn't until some 18 years later I can admit that to myself. I self-stigmatise. I can only now admit to myself why I did it, why I always think about doing it, but why I hopefully will never do it again.

I recently went through two miscarriages – the most emotional last six months of mine and my husband's lives. I didn't self-harm. I thought about it, as I always do, but never had any intention to do it. It was then that I realised I am strong enough to share my story.

All I needed was for someone to support me

I always thought it was my family and friends that showed stigma towards my 'situation' by not really talking about it and sweeping it under the carpet. By alluding to it and making reference to it, but never discussing 'it'. But it wasn't, it was me self-stigmatising. I now realise that it must be a really hard thing for a family member or a friend to see someone clearly struggling and doing so by hurting themselves, and perhaps worrying that that person might go off the rails. From my experience, I know all I needed was for someone to ask me, to support me, to love me and then give me time to reflect on the reasons why.

Hi, my name is Suzi and I am a self-harmer... I intend to be cut free forever.

10 January 2013

The above information is reprinted with kind permission from Time to Change.

www.time-to-change.org.uk 

Coping with self-harming urges

Deliberate self-harm is a behaviour distinct from attempting suicide. For some people it becomes a 'coping strategy' for dealing with overwhelming or painful feelings. Coping with the urges to self-harm requires learning different ways to deal with these feelings.

STUDENTS AGAINST DEPRESSION .ORG

Read with caution

This information has been provided to allow you to think constructively about your self-harming behaviour. However, if you are aware that reading about self-harm practices might feel 'triggering' for you then make sure you read this with someone else present or find another way to reduce the risk.

Work on things step by step

If self-harming has become a kind of coping strategy, it is not usually helpful to focus on completely stopping or banning the behaviour in one sudden step. Instead, it is helpful to build new strategies for dealing with difficult feelings which can gradually take the place of self-harm. In the first instance it can be useful to consider learning first aid and knowing how to take care of yourself practically if you do self-harm.

Creating a personal self-harm safety plan is a useful way to remind yourself of things you can do when you feel an urge to self-harm. These include ways to manage and reduce self-harming behaviours in the short term, so that they are less damaging, as well as alternative ways to manage difficult feelings which can replace self-harm in the longer term.

De-escalate the intensity of self-harm

A first step can be to think about trying to slowly reduce the damage caused by your self-harming behaviour (e.g. cutting less deeply). Then try to move to less damaging practices like writing on your skin with red felt tip instead of cutting.

Direct the harming urge at something else

Some people find squeezing an ice cube provides an alternative that is helpful. Hit pillows or cushions. Flick an elastic band on your wrist. Take a cold bath or shower.

Make a list of distractions

Make a list of activities that you can use to distract yourself. Trying to be with other people is particularly effective.

Know your triggers and reduce the risks

Knowing what kinds of situations are particularly risky for you can help you plan to reduce the risks. For example, it is harder to manage your feelings effectively when you are under the influence of drugs or alcohol. Go easy on these if you are aware that you are feeling less stable.

Learn to tune in to your feelings

In the longer term you can start to learn how to identify the experiences and feelings which are most likely to trigger your urges to self-harm. Learning the skill of 'mindfulness' – being tuned in to what you are feeling in the present moment, without judgement or attempt to change it – is invaluable in the move towards being able to manage or 'ride out' difficult feelings, rather than trying to eliminate them.

Find constructive outlets for feelings

Having a good cry is the natural way to get rid of built up stress hormones and get feelings out. Experiment with different ways to express feelings when they seem to be building up inside, to see what works for you. Keeping a diary can be a useful habit for getting feelings 'out'. Just write it all down without censorship, then close it and put it away. Or it might be helpful to do something symbolic like writing it all down then scribbling it out or tearing it up. Vigorous activity or exercise can be another helpful way to get rid of pent up feelings.

Learn how to self-soothe

Make a conscious effort to take care of yourself and comfort yourself with difficult feelings. Try out different things to see what you find most comforting. Breathing and relaxation exercises can be very useful. A relaxing soak in a bubble bath, hugs or a massage, eating something sweet (in moderation), stroking a pet, listening to uplifting music, knitting or crafts... find what works for you!

Get support and professional help

Having people you can talk to and a good support network is a vital protection against both self-harm and suicidal thinking.

Talking about the inner feelings that fuel your self-harm is potentially useful whoever you talk to, but counsellors are professionally trained to work with self-harm and will be best placed to support you in finding constructive alternatives.

The above material is from studentsagainstdepression.org, a project of the Charlie Waller Memorial Trust. Intellectual property rights for the site are owned by Dr Denise Meyer. We are grateful to the Trust for allowing us to use their material.

www.studentsagainstdepression.org 

Treatments for self-harming

By Beth Morrisey

There is no single treatment that is guaranteed to work in all cases of self-harming. This also applies to cases in which an individual inflicts behaviours such as cutting, burning, head banging, hair pulling and even poisoning on his or her own body. Instead, a combination of treatments geared towards protecting the self-harmer's physical and mental health is often employed to treat self-harmers and help them cease their damaging behaviours. If a self-harmer is in need of medical treatment, this will usually be organised first to makes sure that there is no threat to the individual's life. When the individual's physical health has stabilised, treatment then usually begins to address the individual's mental and/or emotional health as well. In severe cases, residential treatment may be encouraged so that the individual can receive care and attention around the clock. There are several institutions across the United Kingdom that can provide this type of treatment as needed.

Medical treatment

It has been estimated that up to 10% of admissions to hospital wards in the United Kingdom are the result of self-harming behaviours, although since cases of overdose and other substance abuse/misuse are often included in these counts the statistics do become a little blurred. If, however, a self-harmer hurts him or herself to such an extent that medical attention is needed, this medical care will be given before any other type of treatment is explored to address the root causes of self-harming. Cleaning and treating wounds and burns, and investigating for bruises, broken bones and/or tissue damage are common means of providing care for cases of self-harm. Most self-harming behaviours are not done with suicidal intent; however some hospitals may choose to keep individuals who have self-harmed under observation just to be safe. When the individual's physical health has stabilised, counselling and/or therapy is usually then encouraged.

Counselling

Self-harming is often related to conditions such as depression, low self-esteem, feelings of powerlessness and feelings of being overwhelmed. When the root cause of self-harming behaviours is actually emotional, then this basis must be addressed. Traditional counselling, sometimes known as talk therapy, allows those who engage in self-harming behaviours to talk through their emotions and their decisions to self-harm. The counsellor or therapist involved will likely be a source of support for the self-harmer, and a behaviour modification approach may be able to teach self-harmers how to make more healthy choices in the future. If clinical depression is diagnosed, medication may be prescribed, but there is no medication that simply stops self-harming behaviours.

Residential treatment

Both public and private residential facilities exist in the United Kingdom to help treat individuals who engage in self-harming behaviours. Though all types of self-harm are unhealthy, the individual involved will usually need to engage in these behaviours repeatedly for a long period of time, or engage in them to such an extent that there is a risk of long-term health effects or even death before residential treatment options are broached. The Cassel Hospital (Surrey), Althea Park Specialist Service (Gloucestershire) and the Crisis Recovery Unit, Bethlem Royal Hospital (Kent) are but a few of the institutions offering residential treatment for self-harmers.

11 June 2013

DID YOU KNOW

Residential treatment centres

These centres provide a safe environment for people struggling with serious problems. Sometimes referred to as 'rehab' (short for rehabilitation), residential treatment centres are live-in health care facilities which provide professional support and therapy.

Some people may find comfort and understanding being with other people who have first-hand experience of what they're going through, as well as having expertly trained staff dedicated to their care.

www.teenissues.co.uk

Lack of mental health services for children leaves them at risk of suicide and self-harm

New mental health charity launches online counselling support for young people.

One in five children* have symptoms of depression, and almost a third (32%) have thought about or attempted suicide before they were 16. That's according to a report from the new mental health charity, MindFull, being launched today by the team behind BeatBullying.

The new charity will give 11- to 17-year-olds immediate access to free online professional counselling support and advice. The launch is supported by Ed Miliband MP and clinical psychologist Professor Tanya Byron.

The report, *Alone with my thoughts,* includes a survey by YouGov of over 2,000 young people which reveals that nearly a third (29%) have self-harmed because they feel 'down'. Over half (52%) of those who had shown signs of depression as children felt let down by their experiences of mental health support. On average, those children who showed symptoms of depression and talked to more than one person, ended up speaking to people 22 times before they got help. Almost half (47%) of young people with depression never got the help they wanted.

Emma-Jane Cross, CEO and founder of MindFull (part of The BB Group) said:

'Too many children who try to speak out about the way they're feeling are being let down or simply ignored. It's unacceptable that so many are having to resort to harming themselves on purpose in order to cope, or worse still are thinking about ending their own lives. Early intervention is proven to help prevent adult mental health problems, so swift action must be taken now if we are to avoid a legacy of serious long-term mental illness.

'MindFull is a direct result of the feedback that we have been given by thousands of young people in the UK, who tell us they want the flexibility and convenience of an online service.'

MindFull will give children and teenagers the support of mental health professionals and enable them to mentor one another in a safe space. The charity will also educate young people about how to cope with mental health issues – providing information, advice and guidance, both online and through training in schools.

Negative thoughts and feelings have a huge impact on children's lives. The survey shows that over a third (39%) of children said they had found it hard to leave the house because they felt down, and almost one in five (18%) young people say they have felt constantly on edge in the last two weeks. Over a third (38%) of those who had showed signs of depression as children said they had run away from home.

Jessica was 14 when she started to feel very down. She didn't tell anyone about the way she was feeling until she was 15, and even though she started to have suicidal thoughts it took her six months before she was able to talk to her mum and get help.

'People don't understand the effect that depression has on you – I hate it when people dismiss it as simply teenage angst. Some days I feel so low it can be a struggle to do things that I normally love, like reading and writing. We desperately need more education about mental health issues so young people can spot the signs early.

'My generation is constantly online – it's where we look for information and advice, which is why I think a site like MindFull will make an enormous difference to all the young people who feel like they have no one to turn to.'

Children are most likely to speak to their friends about mental health issues, underlining the importance of peer support. Of those that spoke to someone, most confided in a friend (57%), followed by parents (54%) and a face-to-face counsellor (32%). Just 2% of young people said medicine alone is the best way to treat mental health issues, and over two-thirds (68%) think that putting mental health services online would be an effective way to tackle mental health issues among young people.

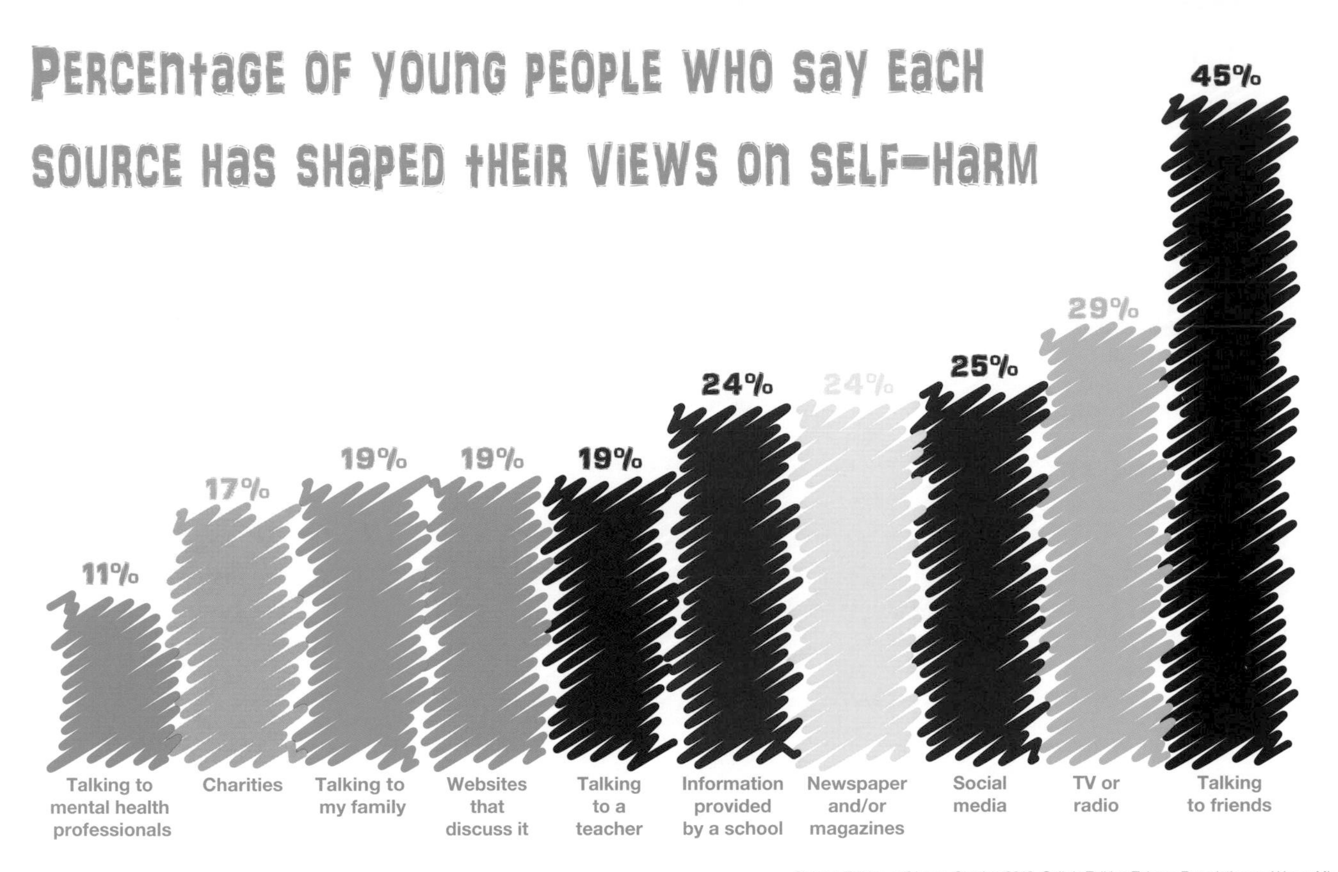

Source: Talking self-harm, *October 2012, Cello's Talking Taboos Foundation and YoungMinds.*

Professor Tanya Byron, President of The BB Group and Chartered Clinical Psychologist said:

'Just as we look after our children's physical health, it's vital that we also offer support for their mental well-being. Children and young people are clearly not getting the help they need, that's why this new online support from MindFull is so important. Teenagers naturally look to the Internet as a source of information and advice, so that's where we need to be in order to help the hundreds of thousands of young people who are currently getting no support.'

The survey also reinforces the need for more information and training in schools. Nearly two-thirds of young people believe adding information on mental health to the national curriculum and training teachers would be effective ways to tackle the problem.

MindFull is calling for mental health to be embedded as a core theme in the national curriculum and for schools to provide access to counselling and mentor support for all young people who need it.

*All figures, unless otherwise stated, are from YouGov plc.

5 July 2013

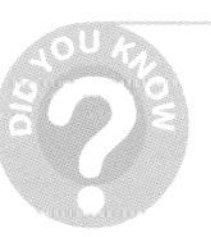

According to figures from two of Britain's biggest NHS mental health trusts, in the last five years a worrying 4,391 children aged ten or under have received treatment for stress, anxiety or depression.

Source: Generation Stress: Scandal of our depressed kids as thousands of under-10s are treated for mental health problems, *Daily Mirror, 10 February 2014.*

www.mindfull.org

Activities

Brainstorm

1. Why do some people self-harm?
2. What help is available for people who self-harm?

Oral activities

3. How do you think the media portrays people who self-harm? Try to think of examples from television, films and even books. Share your ideas and discuss as a class.
4. Look at the graph about the misunderstood statements that parents, teachers and GPs believe about self-harm among young people (page 1) and, as a class, discuss the myths and facts surrounding self-harm.

Research activity

5. Visit Stephen Fry's website (www.stephenfry.com) and research his work with the mental health charity Mind. Do you think it is a good thing for celebrities such as Stephen Fry to speak out about mental illness? Write a one-page essay or a blog post exploring this question.

Written activities

6. Write a guide for parents, giving advice about what they can do if they have a son/daughter who self-harms.
7. Create an informative presentation about how to cope with self-harm and the different options for treatment for self-harming. You might find *Coping with self-harming urges* (page 11) and *Treatments for self-harming* (page 13) helpful.

Moral dilemma

8. You've noticed that your friend Oli has been self-harming. He says that it's a way of coping with his problems. What do you do?

Design activities

9. Design an app that could help people who self-harm. You might want to include things like self-help techniques or where a person can go get support.
10. Design an information booklet that could be distributed throughout your school, or college, to raise awareness of the issues surrounding self-harm. Use the articles in Chapter One to help you.

Suicide

Around 4,400 people end their own lives in England each year – that's one death every two hours – and at least ten times that number attempt suicide.

Around 75% of suicides are men and in almost all cultures, the suicide rate rises with age. The highest rates of suicide in the UK are among people aged over 75 and it remains a common cause of death in men under the age of 35.

Risk factors

Certain factors are known to be associated with increased risk of suicide. These include:

- drug and alcohol misuse
- unemployment
- social isolation
- poverty
- poor social conditions
- imprisonment
- violence
- family breakdown.

People with a diagnosed mental health condition are at particular risk. Around 90% of suicide victims suffer from a psychiatric disorder at the time of their death.

Those at the highest risk of suicide are people suffering from alcoholism, clinical depression or schizophrenia. Previous suicide attempts are also an indication of particular risk. Up to 20% of survivors try again within a year, and as a group they are 100 times more likely to go on to complete suicide than those who have never attempted suicide.

For young people, bullying, family turmoil, mental health problems, unemployment and a family history of suicide can play a part in increasing the risk of suicide. Amongst the young, 80% of suicides are male, and one in three young people who take their lives are intoxicated at the time of death.

For older people, poverty, poor quality housing, social isolation, depression and physical health problems are factors which can increase the risk of suicide. Over 1,000 men aged 50+ end their own lives every year in England and Wales.

Prevention

Feeling suicidal is often a temporary state of mind. If appropriate and timely help and emotional support is offered to people who are experiencing deep unhappiness and distress, this can reduce the risk of them choosing to end their own life.

Following a focused campaign in recent years, numbers of suicides among younger men aged 25 to 34 – previously the highest – have fallen.

There are often certain signs before an attempt at suicide. These can include evidence of self-harm on purpose and the person in question expressing their thoughts in the year before the act to relatives, partners, peers or professionals. These offer potential opportunities to step in and save lives.

Despite this, three-quarters of all people who end their own lives are not in contact with mental health services.

Prevention of suicide is not the exclusive responsibility of any one sector of society. Schools can create cultures in which young people feel it is healthy to talk through emotional and other difficulties. General practitioners can restrict the number of tablets prescribed to those at risk of overdose. Accident and Emergency staff can ensure all young people who have attempted suicide receive specialist mental health assessment. And each of us can pay close attention to the overall mental health of our loved ones to reduce the risks of them taking their lives.

Recovery from a suicide attempt

The attitudes we hold toward people who attempt to take their lives can influence the course of their condition. The isolation that suicidal people feel can be reinforced by a judgemental approach in which their behaviour is viewed as manipulative or selfish. By stepping beyond our personal assumptions, and showing care and respect for the people behind the behaviours, we can help them talk about their feelings and help prevent suicide taking place.

The above information is reprinted with kind permission from the Mental Health Foundation.

www.mentalhealth.org.uk

Suicide: the 's' word

Suicide. There is something about that word that strikes fear in the strongest of people, stirs stigma in those that seem so savvy when it comes to mental health. I am sad to say, I am one of those people.

I find myself talking about mental health on a near daily basis. I write blogs, articles, speak to others, educate anyone and everyone that will listen about the trials and tribulations of living in the shadows of society when you have a mental health condition. In spite of this, I find myself rarely mentioning the 's' word. Despite having gone through an 's' situation myself.

Five years ago, I had a complete mental breakdown. I went from smiley and successful to housebound and horrified in the space of 24 hours. My life changed over night. I found myself on waiting lists, taking medication I didn't really understand, completely alone, with no-one to talk to and no-one who understood.

To this day, I stand by the idea that finding yourself with a mental health condition is a sure-fire way of weeding out the so-called associates that masquerade as 'mates' until you really need a shoulder to cry on.

I dropped to a level of depression that I barely knew existed. The world passed by without me in it, slipping away day by day, and I couldn't imagine me ever being a part of it again.

I took what I thought and felt at the time was a 'rational' decision. I cancelled meetings, social commitments, I said goodbye, I wrote letters. Fortunately one true friend at the time realised what was happening and ensured I was rushed to A&E to ensure my safety.

Even typing out the details, its hard for me to look back on. I feel ashamed, embarrassed. It feels like it happened to a whole other person. But it didn't. It happened to me. A depressed, in need of help and support with nowhere to turn or talk to, me.

It's always at this point I tell myself off. Talking about suicide shouldn't feel embarrassing. Nor should I be ashamed of something so serious. Something that is a 'something' that needs support and so much understanding. My views of 'reality' at the time were so messed up and misconstrued. I was ill. Very ill indeed. And that isn't my fault. It was something that needed treatment and counselling. But due to the stigma, I kept silent – rather than speaking out for the support I so desperately needed.

I shouldn't be ashamed of something that affects so many. Suicide shouldn't be a dirty word, yet of all mental health 'words' it seems to be the dirtiest of all.

If by speaking out I can stop the stigma attached to suicide, then this is worth every difficult sentence and syllable.

World Suicide Prevention Day is about understanding, awareness and, most importantly, helping those hiding away in need of help they so thoroughly deserve. There is support out there and people who understand. There is a way out. There is a light at the end of the ever-darkening tunnel. It's knowing in which direction you need to look.

In those moments when you (or someone you love) feel so alone and afraid, with the grips of debilitating depression slowly squeezing the life from you, remember there are people out there that can hold your hand, people that can help, people that can tell you that yes, things will be OK. This doesn't have to be the end of your story.

Let us all speak out, and start being more honest with each other and most importantly – ourselves. Because by doing so, it's not just our own endings that we can re-write, but it will end the story of stigma attached to suicide – hopefully writing it out of the long-term picture altogether.

And that would be a very happy ending indeed.

10 September 2013

www.mind.org.uk

Mini glossary

Debilitating – *when something is debilitating it seriously affects someone so much that they physically and mentally feel like they can't do anything anymore.*

If you have been thinking about taking your own life or have tried to harm yourself, please read on...

Why do you feel like this?

Lots of young people feel suicidal at some point in their lives. Thousands go into hospital each year having tried to harm themselves. Many more than this attempt to take their own lives – and nobody ever gets to know about it.

The good news is that most recover and never try again. A small number, however, do go on to kill themselves – in the UK about 1,600 young people under the age of 35 each year die because of suicide.

What happens if you go ahead with suicide?

Sometimes the person who attempts suicide does not die but damages their body so badly that full recovery is impossible.

If you take your own life, there is no turning back, no second chance. Death is final.

It can be extremely traumatic for the person who finds your body. Something they will never forget.

The effect of suicide on family and friends can be overwhelming. Of all the different ways of dying, suicide is the most difficult to deal with for those who are left behind – whether they are parents, children, partners, brothers, sisters, friends or even acquaintances.

You won't be around to help other people who may be feeling just as bad as you have done.

You have prevented other people from helping you – forever.

So what can you do about it?

1. Share it

Tell someone else how you are feeling – a member of your family, your doctor, a teacher, school nurse, college counsellor, friend, someone from your church ... If the person you are telling doesn't seem to understand, don't

be put off – tell someone else. Phone the PAPYRUS helpline HOPELineUK 0800 068 41 41. Our staff are there to help. Your call is confidential and you don't have to disclose your identity.

If you reach a suicidal crisis where the desire to kill yourself is overwhelming, you must tell someone. Ask them to keep you company until the feelings pass.

If you find it difficult to talk, write it down – send a letter, an e-mail or a text.

Use the Internet wisely by going only on websites that give positive help and hope for the future. Be very careful when speaking to people in chatrooms – you may be encouraged to go ahead and take your own life.

2. Deal with bad thoughts

Thinking bad thoughts about yourself all the time (especially about killing yourself) makes you feel worse. You might be thinking that you're a failure or nobody likes you or that nothing will get better. There might be some thoughts that are very private to you.

Tell someone you trust about your bad thoughts. Saying them out loud for the first time is scary but they will become less frightening the more you speak about them.

Try to recognise when your bad thoughts are likely to come and prepare for them. Try to find something that will get rid of them or will make you think about them less often. You could try being active, being with people or doing something you enjoy (even though you might not feel like it).

Think about the good things you've done today – instead of the bad things. Some people find that it helps to imagine having a great time with their favourite band or football team or movie star. Or it could be eating your favourite meal or lying on a beach in the sun...

Just thinking about your bad thoughts a bit less often can be a great achievement. It can help you realise that you are starting to win the battle.

3. Get specialist help

Don't be afraid of going to see a specialist such as a counsellor or psychiatrist. You may want to take someone with you for company. Your family and friends can be very important in helping you get through this – think about allowing them to get involved in your treatment. There are some very good 'talking treatments' which work really well, especially if you go in the early days of feeling unwell. If you are not able to relate to the person you are seeing – ask to see someone else.

Listen to the advice you are being given and act on it.

Try to get help with the problems that may be causing your depression. Our helpline staff can give you contact numbers for many national and local sources of additional help.

4. Understand your medication

If you have been given medication (tablets) to help with your suicidal feelings, make sure you understand how long it takes before they start having an effect. If they don't seem to be working, tell your doctor so they can try something else. Don't stop taking them because you feel better or because you are having side effects. Get advice from your doctor first. You can also talk to the pharmacist about your medication.

5. Steer clear of alcohol and drugs

Although at first they give you a lift, they can make depressed people feel even worse in the long run. Under their influence you may do things or make decisions you would not normally make. Using alcohol and/or other drugs – including cannabis – can actually make some people suicidal.

6. Don't take risks

You may be feeling ambivalent about whether you live or die. In this frame of mind people sometimes take chances and do things on purpose which put their lives at risk, for example; driving the car in a way that could kill you (or someone else) or not taking an essential medication. Don't be pressured by other people into doing risky things either.

Be aware of the danger of making an impulsive, spur of the moment decision to kill yourself. This is more likely if something upsetting happens which you feel is the 'last straw', if you are angry or if you've been drinking or taking drugs.

Don't listen to sad music when you're really down. Playing it over and over again can compound suicidal feelings.

7. Take positive action

It may require huge effort but start looking after yourself with regular meals and plenty of exercise. Get out into the daylight and try to stay out of bed until night time. Find something to do which gives some structure to your day.

Make a list, with phone numbers, of people and/or organisations you can turn to for help in a crisis. Store the numbers in your mobile.

The PAPYRUS helpline HOPELineUK 0800 068 41 41 is there to help you. We know that some people find it difficult to pick up the phone. Please call – you have nothing to lose and everything to gain.

Don't expect to feel OK all at once.

Just knowing that life is slowly getting better means there is light at the end of the tunnel.

The above information is reprinted with kind permission from PAPYRUS Prevention of Young Suicide.

www.papyrus-uk.org

Making sense of suicide

Suicide is a highly emotive subject, still often treated as taboo in most cultures. This means that even though it is fairly common, of all the forms of depressed thinking, suicidal thinking is least likely to be aired, discussed and critically evaluated.

STUDENTS AGAINST DEPRESSION .ORG

Deadly tunnel vision

Isolation and painful despair in conjunction with depressed thinking habits make for a very risky combination. Suicidal thinking often arises out of hopelessness about being able to overcome difficult life problems. When someone is desperate for relief from suffering, yet stuck in tunnel vision at the bottom of the depression habit spiral, they are less able to apply problem-solving skills and are vulnerable to the deadly over-simplification of suicidal thinking. The taboo over discussing suicide also means that thinking about suicide can leave someone feeling very isolated and alone.

So how do we make sense of suicide?

Several different paths of thought can lead in the direction of suicide. All are distorted by the narrowed perspective of depressed thinking habits:

'How bad am I feeling?'

People often first think about suicide not so much as an immediate option, but more as a kind of 'barometer' to measure how bad they're feeling. When you are feeling very low, it can seem comforting to recognise that you do not feel quite low enough to commit suicide. This is a very risky habit, because repetition of the thought brings a seemingly comforting familiarity and dulls the initial instinctive recoil from danger.

'Am I a coward or a hero?'

Debate over whether suicide is heroic or cowardly is another irrelevant over-simplification. This kind of all-or-nothing thinking diverts attention from more complex solutions to the problems which have led to the suicidal thinking in the first place.

'I've got to sort it out on my own'

An over-emphasis on individualism, common in Western cultures, creates barriers to help-seeking. Over-valuing 'independence' means that when someone can't find their own solution to their problems suicide becomes the only 'answer'. Yet many people can be, and have been, helped to survive suicidal thinking and overcome depression.

'Won't they be better off without me?'

One angle on suicide focuses on its self-sacrificial aspect, not wanting to be a burden. Yet the distorted perspective of believing that 'they'll be better off without me' tends to be greeted with stunned bewilderment and terrible pain by those who will supposedly be 'better off'. The anguish of a parent who has lost a child to suicide is almost indescribable.

'I'll show them!'

For some, the desire to cause this pain and bewilderment, or at least to have people take them seriously, is a strong motivation. This is the ultimate in cutting off your nose to spite your face – again an over-simplified solution to the complex problem of engaging in meaningful relationships.

Copycat suicide

It is an unfortunate phenomenon that one suicide can sometimes seem to create a kind of domino effect, sparking off a series of suicides in the affected community. More commonly, a suicide in the community is shocking enough to jolt support networks into action for others.

'What's the point to life anyway?'

Pervading cynicism in modern societies creates a strongly depression-inducing cultural context. Cynicism denigrates all that is constructive and hopeful and drains away the meaning from life. Depression and suicidal thinking thrive in the space left when people stop investing hope in their lives.

To be or not to be?

The famous 'To be or not to be...?' speech in Shakespeare's play Hamlet reminds us of another aspect to thinking about suicide. It reflects the strong tradition in many cultures of contemplating death as a way of bringing into focus the value of life.

Depression and the meaning of life

Pain, suffering and the inevitability of death are profoundly difficult issues not just for individuals but for all of humanity.

Surviving suicidal thoughts

A risky habit

Suicidal intentions are prompted by a desperate need for relief from intensely painful feelings. Surviving suicidal thoughts is about learning how to find relief without resorting to suicide.

Simply having suicidal thoughts does not mean you will act on them. However, the habit of repeatedly thinking about suicide is a risky one. Repetition brings a sense of falsely comforting familiarity. It dulls the instinctive recoil from danger. Though it may be difficult, hold on to the belief that there ARE ways to resist depression and find relief.

Tell someone how you're feeling
Tell someone else how you are feeling or get someone to be with you. Be prepared for non-professionals to be shocked by what you tell them, and don't expect a 'perfect' response – it is always better to make human contact than to stay isolated and alone with your thoughts.

Reduce the risks
Protect yourself from impulsively acting on your thoughts by putting dangerous objects out of immediate reach. Preferably give pills, weapons, etc. to someone else for safe-keeping, but even putting them in a locked or inaccessible place makes it a little harder to act impulsively.

Make a commitment to yourself
When you notice thoughts of suicide, challenge the self-bullying habit and make a commitment to taking care of yourself as best you possibly can for the moment. Remind yourself to follow your safety plan if you have made one.

Making a safety plan
A safety plan helps you plan ahead for the times when you may feel particularly low and at risk of acting on your suicidal thoughts. It is a way to personalise and summarise the possible strategies for taking care of yourself.
A safety plan supports your healthier self – the bit of you that wants to hold on and survive – when things are hard and you are feeling overwhelmed. The strategies listed here offer a solid foundation for creating a safety plan and for working towards breaking the suicidal thinking habit.

Attend to your self-care needs
Suicidal thoughts arise as a result of deeply painful feelings of despair and hopelessness. Recognise the pain you are feeling as something which needs a compassionate and caring response. Practise constructive ways to take care of yourself when you are feeling this way.

Plan to get professional help
It is unreasonable to see suicide as the only solution if you haven't sought any professional help for your depression and suicidal thinking. Doctors and counsellors help many people move on from depression and get appropriate help. You may need to challenge yourself about what's stopping you getting help.

Check medication side effects
Be aware that some anti-depressant medication can increase the risk of suicidal thinking, especially when you first start taking them. Also, when the medication first starts taking effect it can increase your energy and motivation before improving your mood, increasing the risk of acting on suicidal thoughts. Talk to your doctor about the risks and be extra vigilant with other strategies for keeping yourself safe.

Check alcohol and drugs
Both alcohol and drugs tend to reduce your inhibitions and make it more likely you could do something you will regret the next day. Check your alcohol/drug consumption and try to cut down. Try not to drink alone or to end up alone after drinking.

Start breaking the suicidal thinking habit
We can't stop thoughts from entering our heads, but we can stop actively inviting them in. Try to stop using thoughts of suicide as a barometer for how bad you are feeling. Use self-soothing or distraction techniques when you notice thoughts about suicide bothering you, or practise other techniques for challenging depressed thinking.

Minimise time spent alone
Depression and suicidal thinking thrive in isolation. Try to minimise time spent alone in your room – take work to the library, ask friends to be with you at vulnerable times, make plans ahead for weekends and other lonelier times, generally work on building your support networks.

Understand some of the reasons for suicidal thinking
Because suicide is such a taboo, you may not be aware of how common it is for people to think about suicide and of the various general reasons for suicidal thinking.

Identify depressed thinking habits
Suicidal thinking is the ultimate all-or-nothing thinking habit, and the culmination of other habits of depressed thinking which intensify the depression habit spiral. Learn more about identifying and challenging depressed thinking, particularly self-bullying.

Work on rebuilding meaning in your life
Depression works to drain assumed meaning out of life and challenges us to take responsibility for making our lives meaningful. Challenge the cynicism or perfectionism which may be preventing you from embracing hopeful or constructive ideals and goals for your life.

Give yourself small goals
Each evening set yourself small tasks or goals for the next day. It can be something as simple as watching a certain TV programme. Or set yourself another task as soon as you have completed one. Just knowing you can still do things you set for yourself despite feeling low can help combat depression.

The above material is from studentsagainstdepression.org, a project of the Charlie Waller Memorial Trust. Intellectual property rights for the site are owned by Dr Denise Meyer. We are grateful to the Trust for allowing us to use their material.

www.studentsagainstdepression.org

UK suicide rate amongst males reaches ten-year high in 2011 and overall number rises 'significantly'

The male suicide rate in Britain hit its highest level in nearly a decade in 2011 whilst the overall number of people taking their own life in Britain increased 'significantly'.

A total of 6,045 suicides were recorded among people aged 15 and over, the Office for National Statistics (ONS) said on Tuesday, up 437 or 8% on the previous year.

The number of male suicides increased 8% to 4,552, which at a rate of 18.2 per 100,000 was the highest level since 2002.

Female suicides also rose 8% to 1,493 or a rate of 5.6 per 100,000.

Two reports last year looked into the reasons behind suicides in the UK.

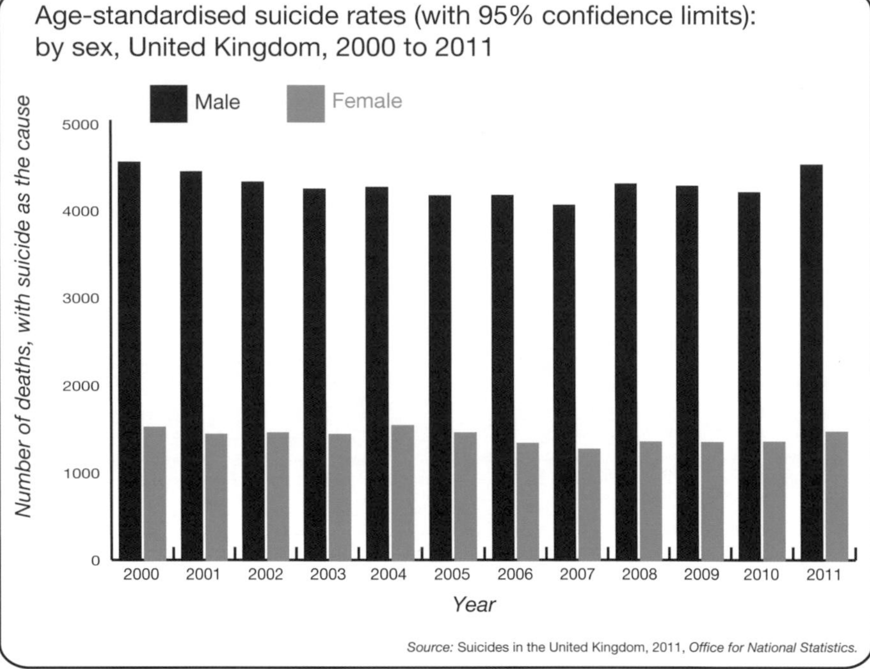

One, by sociologists from Cambridge University, attributed 1,000 suicides to 'economic recession, rising unemployment and biting austerity measures' from 2008-10.

Another by the Samaritans, explored the reasons for suicide beyond mental health problems among middle-aged men and found a loss of masculine pride and identity can tip them over the edge, leaving them more likely to commit suicide.

It found that on average about 3,000 middle-aged men from disadvantaged backgrounds take their own lives each year.

Last year the Government announced a further £1.5 million in funding for research into suicide prevention among those most at risk of taking their own lives.

The pledge came as ministers unveiled a new suicide prevention strategy which aims to cut the suicide rate and provide more support to bereaved families.

The overall suicide rate in the UK increased from 11.1 to 11.8 per 100,000, the ONS said, while the highest suicide rate was among men aged 30 to 44 at 23.5 deaths per 100,000.

Among women, the highest rate of suicide was among 45 to 59-year-olds at 7.3 per 100,000.

In 2011, additional guidance was given to improve the classification of narrative verdicts at inquests in England and Wales.

A narrative verdict is a long-form, factual record of how and in what circumstances a death occurred and is used as an alternative to short-form verdicts such as suicide.

There had been concerns among researchers that these classification rules forced the ONS to record probable suicides as accidents.

So in 2011, the ONS identified common phrases used by coroners to terms allowed for the classification of intentional self-harm.

This additional guidance could have resulted in an increased number of narrative verdicts coded as intentional self-harm in 2011, the ONS said, which in turn could have contributed to the increase in the suicide rate.

If you are affected by any of the issues raised call The Samaritans on 08457 90 90 90.

22 January 2013

www.huffingtonpost.co.uk

Consider a text for teen suicide prevention and intervention, research suggests

Adolescents commonly use social media to reach out when they are depressed.

Teens and young adults are making use of social networking sites and mobile technology to express suicidal thoughts and intentions as well as to reach out for help, two studies suggest.

An analysis of about one month of public posts on MySpace revealed 64 comments in which adolescents expressed a wish to die. Researchers conducted a follow-up survey of young adults and found that text messages were the second-most common way for respondents to seek help when they felt depressed. Talking to a friend or family member ranked first.

These young adults also said they would be least likely to use suicide hotlines or online suicide support groups – the most prevalent strategy among existing suicide-prevention initiatives.

The findings of the two studies suggest that suicide prevention and intervention efforts geared at teens and young adults should employ social networking and other types of technology, researchers say.

'Obviously this is a place where adolescents are expressing their feelings,' said Scottye Cash, associate professor of social work at The Ohio State University and lead author of the studies. 'It leads me to believe that we need to think about using social media as an intervention and as a way to connect with people.'

The research team is in the process conducting a study similar to the MySpace analysis by examining young people's Twitter messages for suicidal content. The researchers would like to analyse Facebook, but too few of the profiles are public, Cash said.

Suicide is the third leading cause of death among youths between the ages of ten and 24 years, according to the US Centers for Disease Control and Prevention (CDC).

Cash and colleagues published the MySpace research in a recent issue of the journal *Cyberpsychology, Behavior and Social Networking*. They presented the survey findings at a meeting of the American Academy of Child and Adolescent Psychiatry.

Cash's interest in this phenomenon was sparked in part by media reports about teenagers using social media to express suicidal thoughts and behaviours.

'We wanted to know: is that accurate, or are these isolated incidents? We found that in a short period of time, there were dozens of examples of teens with suicidal thoughts using MySpace to talk to their friends,' she said.

The researchers performed a content analysis of public profiles on MySpace. They downloaded profile pages of a 41,000-member sample of 13- to 24-year-olds from 3–4 March 2008, and again in December 2008, this time with comments included. By developing a list of phrases to identify potential suicidal thoughts or behaviours, the researchers narrowed two million downloaded comments to 1,083 that contained suggestions of suicidality, and used a manual process to eventually arrive at 64 posts that were clear discussions of suicide.

'There's a lot of drama and angst in teenagers so in a lot of cases, they might say something "will kill them" but not really mean it. Teasing out that hyperbole was an intense process,' Cash said. Song lyrics also made up a surprising number of references to suicide, she added.

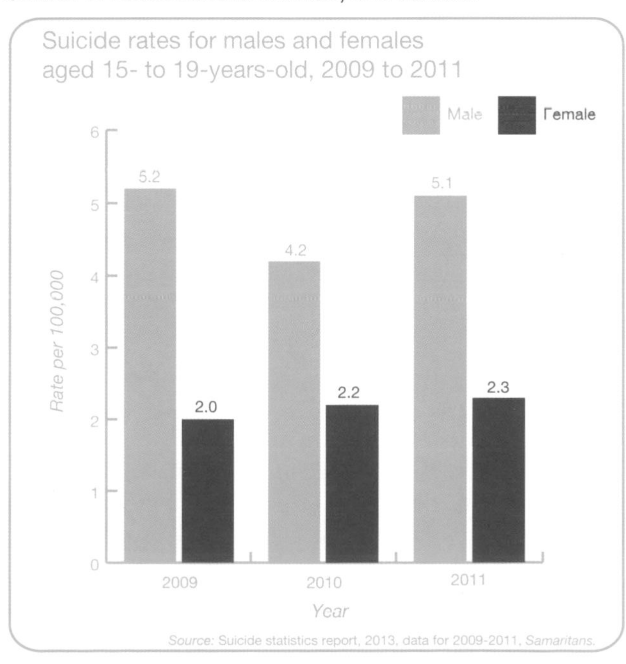

The three most common phrases within the final sample were 'kill myself' (51.6 per cent), 'want to die' (15.6 per cent) and 'suicide' (14.1 per cent). Though in more than half of the posts the context was unknown, Cash and colleagues determined that 42 per cent of the posts referred to problems with family or other relationships – including 15.6 per cent that were about break-ups – and 6.3 per cent were attributable to mental health problems or substance abuse.

Very few of the posts identified the method the adolescents would consider in a suicide attempt, but 3 per cent mentioned guns, 1.6 per cent referred to a knife and 1.6 per cent combined being hit by a car and a knife.

With this information in hand, Cash and co-investigator Jeffrey Bridge of the Research Institute at Nationwide Children's Hospital surveyed young people to learn more about how they convey their depression and suicidal thoughts. Bridge also co-authored the MySpace paper.

Collaborating with Research Now, a social marketing firm, the researchers obtained a sample of survey participants through a company that collects consumer opinions. The final sample included 1,089 participants age 18–24 with an average age of almost 21, half male and half female, and 70.6 per cent white.

They were asked about their history of suicidal thoughts and attempts, general Internet and technology use, social networking activity and whether they had symptoms of depression.

More than a third reported they have had suicidal thoughts; of those, 37.5 per cent had attempted suicide, resulting in a 13 per cent rate of suicide attempts among the entire sample. That figure compares to the eight per cent of US high-school students who reported in a 2011 CDC national survey that they had attempted suicide at least once in the previous year. According to that survey, almost 16 per cent of youths had seriously considered suicide and almost 13 per cent had made a suicide plan in the previous 12 months.

'Obviously this is a place where adolescents are expressing their feelings. It leads me to believe that we need to think about using social media as an intervention and as a way to connect with people.'

Results of Cash's survey showed that respondents would favour talking to a friend or family member when they were depressed, followed by sending texts, talking on the phone, using instant messaging and posting to a social networking site. Less common responses included talking to a health-care provider, posting to a blog, calling a suicide prevention hotline and posting to an online suicide support group.

Response trends suggested, though, that participants with suicidal thoughts or attempts were more willing to use technology – specifically the phone, instant messaging, texting and social networking – to reach out compared to those with no suicidal history. In light of this trend, the fact that the participants were active online consumers might have contributed to the relatively high percentage of suicide attempts among the study sample. In addition, the survey also asked about lifetime suicide history, not just recent history, Cash noted.

The survey also showed that this age group looks to the Internet for information on sensitive topics, and again suggested that young adults of both sexes with a history of suicidal thoughts or attempts consulted the Internet for information about topics that are difficult to discuss – specifically drug use, sex, depression, eating disorders or other mental health concerns. Females with past suicide attempts used social networking the most, according to the results.

'It appears that our methods of reaching out to adolescents and young adults is not actually meeting them where they are. If, as adults, we're saying, 'this is what we think you need' and they tell us they're not going to use it, should we keep pumping resources into suicide hotlines?' Cash said. 'We need to find new ways to connect with them and help them with whatever they're struggling with, or, in other words, meet them where they are in ways that make sense to them.'

A notable resource already available is www.reachout.com, a website geared toward adolescents who are struggling through a tough time. Some Internet-based resources exist that could serve as models for new suicide prevention interventions, she noted. They include teen.smokefree.gov and www.thatsnotcool.com.

The survey research was supported by an Ohio State University College of Social Work Seed Grant.

Additional co-authors of the MySpace paper include Michael Thelwall of the University of Wolverhampton in the United Kingdom, Sydney Peck of Elmira College and Jared Ferrell of the University of Akron.

24 June 2013

www.researchnews.osu.edu

Activities

Brainstorm

1. Are suicide and self-harm related?
2. What should someone do if they start to experience suicidal thoughts?

Oral activities

3. Is suicide a topic that is talked about in schools? Do you think it should be? With a partner, discuss and then share with your class.
4. Why might the recession be a possible factor in the increase in suicide rates? Discuss as a group.

Research activity

5. A recent report from the Samaritans found that male suicide rates have increased. Go to their website and find the report *Men and Suicide, why it's a social issue*. Read the executive summary and then choose one section (personality traits, masculinity, etc.) and read it in full. Create a bullet point list of the things in your chosen section that contribute to male suicide rates and then feedback to your class.

Written activities

6. Read the article *Consider a text for teen suicide prevention and intervention...* (pages 25 and 26). Write a summary of the article for your school newspaper.
7. Read *Making sense of suicide* (pages 21-23) and focus on the 'Making a safety plan' diagram on pages 22 and 23. Write a blog that will give students tips and advice on how to cope with suicidal thoughts and how to create a safety plan.

Moral dilemma

8. With a partner, discuss the steps you could take if a friend confided in you that he/she was experiencing suicidal thoughts.

Design activities

9. Design a poster that will encourage people who may be experiencing suicidal feelings to seek help. Carefully consider how you can promote the issue without sensationalising it.
10. Read *Suicide* (page 17). Create an informative leaflet for your GP's office which highlights the risk factors that are known to be associated with increased risk of suicide.

Key facts

- *About one in ten young people will self-harm at some point, but it can happen at any age. (page 1)*
- *In a recent study of over 4,000 self-harming adults in hospital, 80% had overdosed and around 15% had cut themselves. (page 1)*
- *About three in 100 people who self-harm over 15 years will actually kill themselves. (page 3)*
- *Self-injurers usually do not want to die. When they self-harm, they are not trying to kill themselves – they are trying to cope with their pain. (page 4)*
- *In the Samaritans report* Youth Matters – A Cry For Help *43% of young people knew someone who has self-harmed, but one-in-four didn't know what to say to a friend who was self-harming. (page 6)*
- *Around 25,000 11- to 25-year-olds are admitted to Accident and Emergency each year in England because of self-harming. (page 6)*
- *One in five children have symptoms of depression, and almost a third (32%) have thought about or attempted suicide before they were 16. (page 14)*
- *The report,* Alone with my thoughts, *includes a survey by YouGov of over 2,000 young people which reveals that nearly a third (29%) have self-harmed because they feel 'down'. (page 14)*
- *Research shows that, of children who spoke to someone about mental health, most confided in a friend (57%), followed by parents (54%) and a face-to-face counsellor (32%). (page 14)*
- *Over two-thirds (68%) [of young people] think that putting mental health services online would be an effective way to tackle mental health issues among young people. (page 14)*
- *Around 75% of suicides are men and in almost all cultures, the suicide rate rises with age. (page 17)*
- *The highest rates of suicide in the UK are among people aged over 75 and it remains a common cause of death in men under the age of 35. (page 17)*
- *One in three young people who take their lives are intoxicated at the time of death. (page 17)*
- *The overall suicide rate in the UK increased from 11.1 to 11.8 per 100,000, the ONS said, while the highest suicide rate was among men aged 30 to 44 at 23.5 deaths per 100,000 (2011). (page 24)*
- *Among women, the highest rate of suicide was among 45 to 59-year-olds at 7.3 per 100,000. (2011). (page 24)*
- *Teens and young adults are making use of social networking sites and mobile technology to express suicidal thoughts and intentions as well as to reach out for help. (page 25)*

Glossary

Anxiety – *Feeling nervous, worried or distressed, sometimes to a point where the person feels so overwhelmed that they find everyday life very difficult to handle.*

Copycat suicides – *In rare cases, an individual may choose to take their own life because they have heard about others doing so, or have been exposed to suicide via the media.*

Counselling – *Sometimes known as talk therapy, allows people who self-harm to talk through their emotions and their decisions to hurt themselves. The counsellor or therapist provides support and may be able to teach self-harmers how to make more healthy choices in the future.*

Depression – *When someone is suffering from depression, their feelings and thoughts of sadness or misery don't go away quickly and are so bad that they interfere with everyday life. Symptoms can include low self-esteem and no motivation.*

Group therapy – *These are meetings for people who are seeking help for a problem (in this case, self-harm or suicidal thoughts) and are led by trained specialists who provide professional advice and support.*

Medication – *If a self-harmer is diagnosed with a mental illness such as clinical depression, medication may be prescribed, but there is no medication that simply stops self-harming behaviours.*

Mental health – *Sometimes called 'psychological well-being' or 'emotional health', mental health refers to the state of your mind and how a person can cope with everyday life. It is just as important as good physical health.*

Self-harm/self-injury – *Self-harm is when a person harms their own body on purpose. People injure themselves in many different ways, including cutting, burning, or poisoning. Self-harmers often see harming as a coping strategy and give a variety of motivations for hurting themselves, including relieving stress/anxiety, focusing emotional pain and as a way of feeling in control. It is not usually an attempt to commit suicide, although people who self-harm are statistically more likely to take their own lives than those who don't.*

Self-help groups – *A group of people meet regularly to give each other emotional support and practical advice. Just sharing your problems in a group can help you to feel less alone – others in the group will almost certainly have had similar experiences (in this case, self-harm).*

Suicide – *Suicide is when a person takes their own life. Men are statistically more likely to take their own life than women, and suffering from a mental illness such as depression, bipolar disorder or schizophrenia is also a risk factor for suicide. Elderly people are also considered vulnerable as they are more likely to have to deal with traumatic life events such as bereavement and ill health.*

Trigger – *A trigger is when a situation or something gives someone the need and urge to self-harm themselves. This can be certain words or pictures, especially relating to the act of self-harm.*